MENTAL TOUGHNESS

How To Build A Strong Mindset And Achieve Your Goals

TABLE OF CONTENTS

INTRODUCTION 1

Chapter 1: Mental Toughness Explained 7

Chapter 2: Exercises and Results 22

Chapter 3: Perseverance and Action 38

Chapter 4: Meditation, Visualization and Affirmation 53

Chapter 5: Mental Toughness Techniques 69

Chapter 6: Flexing the Mind 84

Bonus Content 99

© Copyright 2018 by_____
-All rights reserved.

The follow eBook is reproduced below with the goal of providing information that is as accurate and reliable as possible. Regardless, purchasing this eBook can be seen as consent to the fact that both the publisher and the author of this book are in no way experts on the topics discussed within and that any recommendations or suggestions that are made herein are for entertainment purposes only. Professionals should be consulted as needed prior to undertaking any of the action endorsed herein.

This declaration is deemed fair and valid by both the American Bar Association and the Committee of Publishers Association and is legally binding throughout the United States.

Furthermore, the transmission, duplication or reproduction of any of the following work including specific information will be considered an illegal act irrespective of if it is done electronically or in print. This extends to creating a secondary or tertiary copy of the work or a recorded copy and is only allowed with express written consent from the Publisher. All additional right reserved.

The information in the following pages is broadly considered to be a truthful and accurate account of facts and as such any inattention, use or misuse of the information in question by the reader will render any resulting actions solely under their purview. There are no scenarios in which the publisher or the original author of this work can be in any fashion deemed liable for any hardship or damages that may befall them after undertaking information described herein.

Additionally, the information in the following pages is intended only for informational purposes and should thus be thought of as universal. As befitting its nature, it is presented without assurance regarding its prolonged validity or interim quality. Trademarks that are mentioned are done without written consent and can in no way be considered an endorsement from the trademark holder

INTRODUCTION

This book is about how to achieve mental toughness by setting realistic and achievable goals and how these goals are actually reached.

In the following chapters, the reader will become familiar with techniques that serve to obtain mental toughness starting with tailor made affirmations that serve you personally in your quest. Instead of memorizing things you will repeat them over and over again and write them down so you will never forget them.

The most important element in achieving mental toughness is perseverance and action. Perseverance is just another side of concentration and in order to harness this inner strength, the reader will learn to focus in a better way and use tools such as meditation, visualization and focus.

The way to use and strengthen perseverance is to break down abstract principles and turn them into practicable and doable portions of knowledge that can be used to the ends needed in the pursuit of our ultimate goal.

These instruments of knowledge require use and practice and the best way to practice anything is to find an aspect that is pleasing and satisfying. Once the reader masters the basic exercises and learns how to set goals, then achieving them becomes easier.

One thing that must not be forgotten is the psychological element which is that we need to change our point of view about ourselves and accept that we can be successful at something such as mental strength. This is like bodybuilding, one needs to repeat the process over and over again for the "muscle" to become strong, in this case, the muscle is the mind. Practice makes perfect.

In this book the reader will learn:

- What exactly is mental toughness? How do we get it?
- What do we do to get it? Exercises and results.
- Perseverance and action.
- Other ways of visualizing our future mental strength.
- Summary of the techniques explained so far.
- Flexing the mind. Our new mind and how to keep it that way.

This book in 6 chapters has covered the way in which an ordinary person starts to master the basics needed to turn an ordinary mind into an extraordinary mind by means of techniques and practice.

Each chapter covers a different aspect of what is needed in the process of fortifying the mind until it can achieve many things that others would consider extraordinary and we started off with a regular, normal mind. On the way to achieving a superlative mind, the reader will pick up different tools and ways of thinking that serve to make what seems herculean, a normal, ordinary thing. Basic elemental things such as repetition, focusing, visualizing and meditation all serve the reader in his or her quest for mental strength and we did it in the end.

Mental strength is achievable like anything else, by dint of repetition, breakdown into smaller manageable parts.

The goal is there and we start a route to get it. If the reader does all the things in the book and practices and perseveres, he or she will develop a superlative mind that is strong. Nothing is impossible if we break down the elements into sections that can be used to construct a total in the end that will enable us to have a mind that can be set to deal with almost any problem or challenge. The book covers all the necessary steps to reach the ultimate goal and if the reader does all the things in the book, he or she will be able to deal with almost any problem that appears in life.

CHAPTER 1

MENTAL TOUGHNESS EXPLAINED

Plato in his "Republic" talks about mental toughness. The Romans believed that men had to study certain subjects in order to become trained in the best traits of life which included basic intelligence, the right attitude towards things as well as core values. The subjects the Romans believed could bring about this type of mental fortitude were music, geometry, grammar, logic, astronomy, rhetoric and arithmetic. In Greco-Roman times these subjects were studied by rote and imitation. This lasted until quite recently and it was only later when pedagogues decided that this type of education was counter-productive and what was required was a "softer" type of education based on moral values and the humanities studies were brought to the fore, however, we will not deal with this and will deal with the basics about mental toughness which in our times is seeing a resurgence in modern thinking.

Today mathematics is seen to be a mental toughness and the idea is to transpose mathematical thinking to common life thinking and problem solving.

One of the ways to achieve mental toughness is to use mindfulness. This is a type of thinking that means we focus on what we are doing right now down to the finest detail. For example; eating. In mindfulness we would focus first on the table. Look at the table, see what its colors are, if it is wood, glass, iron or plastic. How high the table is? What it measures. What is on the table. The cutlery we are going to use to eat, the dishes, the different sets of dishes and cutlery for the other people that will be eating with us. Then we focus on the food. What exactly are we going to be eating? How we will be eating and we focus on our body, our arm reaching for the fork, the hand that grasps the fork, the fingers that hold it, the hand that goes down reaching for the food, the morsel that is placed on the fork. How the fingers, hand, arm and body move as we place the fork in our mouth with the food. The food. Is it hot or cold? Is it crunchy or soft? Does it drip. Is it salty or sweet? The color of it. The odor of it. We chew it carefully extracting all the nutrition in it. We swallow. We focus all the time on the act of eating and we eat carefully, being and fusing ourselves with the act of nutrition. We are not distracted by other people, tv, a book, the radio, etc. We focus on the act of eating single mindedly. This is mindfulness and it can be applied to everything we do. By practicing mindfulness every day, we can reinforce our willpower and according to scientists, this can actually increase gray matter in the brain.

Willpower is strengthened by mindfulness. Willpower is about the refusal to give in, to cave. Willpower is mindfulness in action. By meditating you create a calm space in your mind where your mind is not leaping from one thing to the next and with willpower you force your mind to stay still in the present. This is not easy. You must have tried meditating from time to time and all it did was two things: you got restless and left the meditation room or else you fell asleep. The way to meditate is to use mindfulness to calm your mind and anchor it to the present. Try to sit still and pay attention to what is happening around you or in you at this precise moment. Don't get distracted. Just sit there and focus on what is happening right now. It is hard. Mental toughness is about doing this every single time you lose focus and this is where willpower comes in. Willpower is what will get you where you want to be every time your attention wanes. The best thing about willpower is that it can be fortified just like your mind because it is like a muscle and you can make it stronger.

Willpower is part of self-discipline. It is the essence of self-discipline. Forcing yourself to do things cannot be done without willpower. Willpower is the grease that the self-discipline machine uses to carry out the motions leading you to a better place inside yourself.

Willpower is what you need to strengthen in order to have mental toughness, it is one of the ingredients you need on your way to a more disciplined mind.

So, we have some things to use now right at the very beginning: mindfulness which is a form of willpower in baby steps. Willpower and these are attitudinal things that we need to use in our quest for mental toughness.

How do we get mental toughness?

There is no easy way to obtain mental toughness. It takes a lifetime to cultivate the mind. It is almost an art (remember the music, one of the subjects of the Romans that Plato talked about?). There is no way to buy yourself mental toughness. The only way is hard work so prepare for that. Make yourself a plan, a scheme, a way to tackle the issue. Use a notebook to write down all the things you will be doing and keep a sort of mental toughness diary. Read it every day.

Maybe you had a falling out in life, maybe something derailed you from your set path you had. Now while you are in your low moment, or contemplative moment, is the time to set the groundwork for your future which starts now (remember, mindfulness). Now is the time to ditch the old you that wasn´t working and get yourself a new you (remember, attitudes). Make yourself abide by a new set of rules. There are ways in which you can use your daily living activities to have more self-discipline. One is getting up early. This doesn´t seem like much but if you include it in your new you, it will make you start the day at a different hour and this in itself is going to have an impact on your day. Try it, if you get up at 8 in the morning, try getting up at 7 and see what the world looks like at that time of day. At first you will need almost all your willpower because when you open your eyes and see that it is still very early, your body will be begging you to snuggle down and stay in bed. Don´t. Get up and take a shower. Get yourself a coffee and once you have overcome the temptation to stay in bed and are actually in the kitchen preparing a coffee or a juice, give yourself a pat on the back. It will get easier as your mind adapts to your new schedule and, now that you have gotten up, what about using this extra hour for something special? Try meditation. Go into your living room or your porch with your coffee. If it is summer, sit out there in mindfulness taking in the sensations of the early morning. Stay out there for an hour, it won´t be wasted. Remember, you are rewarding yourself for having gotten up early and you got up early because you are on your way to having greater mental toughness. You are mapping out the steps you need to achieve your long-term goal and don´t forget to keep the forest in mind while focusing on the trees. This is a sample of what a person can do in an easy way to change his or her life.

Mental toughness is something you can learn but it is necessary to practice and repeat it a lot. This is the downside but if you use mindfulness as a tool, you can practice and repeat endlessly and effortlessly after a while because with mindfulness every time you do it is like the first time and this comes with an added thing, a Zen like quality that makes repetition pleasurable. If you practice a sport you will know what this is: it is hitting the ball perfectly every time like in tennis or the runner´s "high", the surge of dopamine in the brain helping you overcome the grind of repetition. If you make it a habit to observe yourself in a detached way while you are doing your practicing and repetition, you will develop your mindfulness and your self-discipline. There are ways that can help you achieve your self-discipline. One thing is to make it easy on yourself, eliminate things that suck your energy, that detract from your goal, for example, if you were dieting, eliminate the snacks and junk food. This is just common sense. It is not a good idea to go to the supermarket at lunch time. Use your common sense and eliminate the temptations that are going to undermine your self-discipline. If you get up in the morning early, do it. Get up and get away from the bed. Move. Go to the kitchen. Do something so you don´t crawl back into bed.

While considering snacks and junk food, remember to focus on healthy eating. This is part of the Spartan like training you will need to foster your mental- toughness so take it to another level and include proper eating in your routine.

Another element in getting mental toughness is to give yourself prizes for achieving things. Don´t make your quest for mental toughness a Marine training site because you will make things so difficult, so almost impossible to achieve that you will fail. Set yourself easy to achieve goals, gradually make them a little harder and set yourself up to win. This is a difficult thing. Lots of people who have decided to embark on achieving mental toughness to immure them from failure and disappointment do so because they have suffered a lot from failure and disappointment. One of the things to watch out for is the paradoxical thing which is: I fasted for one day and didn´t eat anything. I am great. Then, immediately after, I rush out to McDonalds and have a binge... Why is this? This is because my mental toughness is so green and raw that I cannot withstand success and need to fail. Then we feel miserable and get all despondent and start considering Spartan discipline... this is wrong. The thing to do is to take it in stride.

Make room for failure and remember to immediately get up and start again or rather, continue. This is the key word: continue. The first time you have a major fail, you will throw this book out the window and go to bed feeling miserable because you failed. But if you go out and find this book and dust it off and read it again, the next time you fail will not be as bad. And this is the wonderful thing. Failing starts fading. Winning starts pushing failing to a side and one day during your mindfulness you will notice how you have changed.

Change: This is the secret to staying young forever. Change. The way in which you no longer do the things you used to do and now do new things or different ones. These are things to consider. If you let yourself change. If you are flexible and use your failings to change yourself, you will find ways in which your mental toughness will start having an effect on what you do every day. Experience is mindfulness in action. Mindfulness is mental toughness in action.

When you fail, which you will do, be sure to take note. Be disappointed, frustrated and angry but don´t forget the forest while you bash your head against the tree. Keep the forest in mind and go back. Get up early and dedicate some early morning silence to mindfulness and pick up where you left off. Practice makes perfect and remember, the Greco-Romans prided themselves on rote learning. So, you should too.

CHAPTER 2

EXERCISES AND RESULTS

There are lots of things we can do to get self-discipline. People who go to a gym regularly are engaging in self-discipline. You can be one of them. Go to a gym and sweat and suffer there while you lose weight or get yourself into shape.

Each person is different but the ultimate things remain the same. All the great thinkers and philosophers will stress on self-discipline or hard work or the golden rule but each one of them is and was a totally different person.

When they asked J.S. Bach how he wrote so much music, he looked up and said, "I put in a day's work..." and there are hundreds of others that make humble statements like this. However, you aren't reading this to know what the greats of history had to say about mental toughness. You are reading this because you or someone you know should change and have mental toughness and how to get it.

There are exercises. Early educators believed in tough rote memory exercise, gymnastic exercise, fasting and prayer. Modern thinkers have removed the excess in discipline and pared it down to the essentials so you can get the results you seek in a more precise way.

One very simple way to exercise self-discipline is to make it very simple. Take a notebook with squared sheets and make a square with ten by ten squares so you have one hundred in a box. Sit down and meditate. Breathe correctly and concentrate on what is going on inside your body. Every time you reach a state of awareness and it goes, use a marker and cross out a box in your grid. Go back and focus on your breathing and get yourself back in your state of consciousness and stay there. When it passes and you wake up. Ink out another box in the grid. Don´t worry too much about how long you lasted because the exercise you are disciplining yourself in is reaching the "Zen" stage of mindfulness. It won´t last but if you do this you will notice how it becomes easier and easier to reach the state of consciousness in the meditation. This is a major achievement and after a certain amount of discipline and sticking with it, you will no longer need the grid to stay focused.

Another exercise you will need is visualization. In visualization you "dream" yourself to success. This can work with almost anything you set your mind to, from winning the lottery to overcoming stage fright. What you do is close your eyes and visualize yourself winning the prize, overcoming the stage fright or whatever else it is that you really want but don´t indulge because what you want to be doing is meticulously planning the dream. You want to break it down into small portions that you can visualize and logically chain them together.

A good way to use mindfulness which is the basic way to get yourself into the right mindset to effect change by reinforcing your willpower is to focus on chores. For example, you are a housewife picking up after the kids went off to school and there are hundreds of LEGO pieces all over the playroom area that you, the mother, are going to pick up. Put to one side the anger or irritation caused by careless kids that left you with all the work. Use mindfulness to pick each piece up and clear a space. Focus on your hand picking up the LEGO piece and the clear area that results from tidying up.

Use this focused attention to clean the whole house and while you do this, let yourself feel the emotions you feel about chores or kids that caused this in the first place. You will be surprised at the results. Firstly, you will have been so focused on using mindfulness to tidy up the living room that at the end you will have cleaned the whole house and even forgiven the kids for messing up in the first place.

This is powerful stuff that you will be able to use for many other aspects of life. Use simple things like this to train yourself for harder things like searching for Vacuity in Buddhism. Maybe you don´t believe in Buddhism but a concept like Vacuity is very useful for mindfulness and focusing. Learn to find answers to mental toughness in other areas of knowledge. Music is another way of focusing. When you listen to music try to feel every single note and duration it has. Listen to one sound after the other. Feel with it.

A part of mental toughness is being a little Spartan. Make yourself feel a little pain. When in the gym, go an extra lap when you believe you just can´t. Let yourself feel discomfort because all of this is going to be part of your journey towards mental toughness.

Remember, the Romans believed in Spartan training and you should include a little suffering in order to prepare yourself for the suffering that is part of changing your way of being in order to have greater mental toughness.

The way to see what happens on your path to mental toughness is to check for results. In the beginning, there won´t be many results or there will be bad results. This is why you include Spartan suffering because the bad results will make you feel bad but your mental toughness will help you overcome this suffering and get back on track. The results are the gauge that lets you know how you are doing on your path to self-discipline and mental strength.

Keep a private notebook with your progress. This is vitally important because by keeping a record you will not cave into temptation to quit because you will have it in writing reminding you that there is a possibility of surrendering. You want to stay focused and by keeping a ledger you will be able to view your progress as you go along. Pretend it´s money. Use your ledger as a bank of promise. You can make lists and cross off items. Remember to tick boxes where you are rewarded. For example, you want to lose weight. Well, you can have a grid in your notebook where you cross off the days you did not give in to snacks. Review it. Count the days you succeeded. Count the days left until your reward. Have different types of boxes for different activities. You can have one for work things you achieved, another for studies, etc.

Exercises are ways of testing willpower and mental toughness is made up of willpower to a large degree. Your exercises in your notebook are your personal record of success and as time goes by you will see the negative boxes diminish as the positive achievement ones grow. Exercises such as this will give you a general view of the things you need to do to gain mental toughness. Keep your exercises simple and manageable. Don´t dedicate the entire weekend to mindfulness because the following weekend you won´t want to dedicate ten minutes to it. That is bad. It is better to dedicate ten minutes every day to an exercise than a mammoth session of two hours straight.

Remember that the ultimate goal is to have the mental toughness that will help you get where you want to be in life and these small exercises are training for that. Don´t forget the trees while you are in the woods.

Soon you will start being aware of how far you can go in the exercises and they will start getting easier as you practice them. This is the rote effect from the discipline. You are beginning to have self-discipline! This is a success in a big way. You are beginning to change. But don´t forget that you can still fail and you want to protect yourself from failure as much as possible until it doesn´t matter anymore because you will be a person with great discipline and willpower. By then you will have changed and what bothers you now or what saps your self-discipline and willpower will be different then. Don´t worry about it now. Focus on the here and now of self-discipline.

Mental toughness includes good things such as your virtues, kindness, patience, generosity, solidarity and love. Be sure to include these in your set of positive emotions that form part of your new way of being that is being sculpted by your daily actions of mental toughness and willpower.

Your emotions will affect your willpower and your mental toughness. Keep them under control so as not to give in to emotions negative or positive that could side-step you from your main goal which is reinforcing your mental toughness.

Don´t forget the larger picture which is harnessing your emotions and your energies to guide you to a disciplined approach to living. This does not mean that you don´t feel emotions and are a robot, no, what you don´t do is give in to your emotions and let yourself be swept away by them. You feel them and you express them but they don´t rule you. You don´t repress your emotions.

Various exercises that can be done to strengthen your willpower that will help your self-discipline are things like working on things that are procrastination provoking. For example, the lawn needs mowing. Get up and mow it now because that way you strengthen your willpower by overcoming the resistance to not do that chore.

Another exercise like the above is coming home from work and wanting to lie down on the couch and watch television. Don´t. Put the leash on the dog and take him out for his walk. This will reinforce your willpower and make you feel better in achieving goals.

You can make small sacrifices and do all sorts of things that require willpower and mental toughness.

A special mention for willpower and discipline is quitting smoking. This is a biggie for many people. With willpower and mental toughness, you can quit smoking. If you are able to quit smoking with willpower and mental toughness then you enter the realm of people with proven objective willpower and self-discipline. However, remember to stay humble. It all started with small changes in your daily routine, changes and self-care and protection to not fall and cave in and smoke a cigarette. If you can quit smoking by using self-discipline, you are on the right track for really changing your life.

The rule to go by is to do things you would rather not do because of procrastination, weakness, laziness and if you do them you gradually become stronger because you overcome internal resistance and unwillingness. This makes the mind stronger because it is like physical exercise. The whole time you are doing different types of exercise to get self-discipline and a mental strength.

The right attitude is to change your point of view so you start seeing the challenges of daily living as opportunities to strengthen your willpower and this will make your mental toughness seek out challenges much the same way a weight lifter will add to his load and make it greater. However, these challenges and exercises are not the goals in the end, they are merely a means to an end. The end is to have changed in such a way that you can enjoy life better, seize opportunities as they come and avoid defeat.

The philosophy behind all of this is that we only have one life to live and the only chance we really have is this life and it is up to us to live it as best as we can. We cannot let a single day go by without experiencing it to its utmost. This means no concessions to anything that will get us down or blame others for whatever ails us.

We want our mental toughness to help us live a better life, and all these exercises and things we do to strengthen our willpower are ultimately to live this only life we have, in the best possible way.

CHAPTER 3

PERSEVERANCE AND ACTION

Perseverance is necessary to keep our project alive and prospering. Perseverance will wear down the resistance against change and create the foundations for willpower to act. Perseverance is like an upper layer in the mind that says "Go. Do it". And we then use willpower for that to happen. For example, we decide to get up early every day even when we don´t have to. You will first need to realize that you want to get up early for whatever reason. You will use your mental toughness to make this an active decision and then you will use perseverance to not lose track of this new wish in your life and willpower will get you up in the mornings.

Perseverance is the tool you use to eat away against resistance. Your entire body will be telling you at six a.m. that there is no need to get up so early and all sorts of rationalizations will start happening and you will need your willpower to get you up and then your perseverance to start eroding that part of you that does not want to get up early. Part of perseverance is repetition. The brain has the mechanisms that you instilled in it during many years of not getting up at six a.m. and now you need your perseverance to change that. Sheer willpower won´t work on its own because that is what you can use for one single time, for example, you need to get up at 6 a.m. because you have a flight to catch. Willpower will help you make that one supreme effort.

Perseverance is the tool that you use to repeat over and over again a new thought pattern, a new habit or a new idea. You need to repeat over and over again because the old pattern or habit is already etched into your brain and you need to replace it with a conscious new habit. For example, you want to quit smoking. Willpower alone will keep you from touching that cigarette lying on the table once or twice but it will be a titanic effort, something you will only be wanting to do once or twice. With your perseverance you erode the mental habit you already have and create a new pattern of thinking so you sit there wanting to smoke and thinking about all the reasons you don´t want to smoke and gradually with perseverance, with repetition and tiny doses of willpower you get past the first six hours of the day without smoking. Then you carry on with a new set of thinking patterns to get through the next six hours until bedtime and one more day you beat the urge to smoke, eat, spend money, lie in bed or whatever else it is that you want to overcome.

In a way, perseverance could be considered to be the tool that willpower uses to achieve small steps in a larger goal. In other words, perseverance is a smaller kind of willpower, a tool that is accessible to use whereas willpower is sort of like a master tool. Willpower is kind of vague, all-encompassing mental strength while perseverance is the one-step-at-a-time kind of approach.

The action is another part of this basic way of approaching the major problem of how to strengthen and use willpower. The action is the actual things we do to achieve our goal of greater willpower which will make us have greater mental toughness and, in the end, mental strength. One of the ways to use action is to make a list of the things we want to change about us because don´t forget that one very important thing in this entire process is that we are going to change. Become a different type of person and for that, we need to be extremely flexible and this will mean learning new habits and new ways of thinking. Saying goodbye to your old self is not easy.

There will be many times in which you will "revert to type" and you won´t like it but since it will feel familiar, you will use old forms of thinking to adapt to your old self. Don´t! That is giving up. Change is scary because it is unfamiliar so be sure to know exactly what you want to achieve with change in yourself. How do you want to change? Why. Make a list of the new things and the old things. This is going to be major plastic surgery in your soul. Be sure that what results is what you are looking for and that you are willing to sacrifice and pay the price to get where you want to be.

For example, dieting or going to the gym. Normally people who have decided to diet or go to a gym, think about it a little, visualize themselves trim or fit and then go to the gym. They then last for a month or so and they quit. Why? Because they did not take into account all the variables about change. They didn´t make a list of what would be happening and how they were going to deal with all the imponderables, the good ones and the bad ones. The easy ones and the hard ones.

In your quest for mental toughness to overcome obstacles or reach goals in life, you are attempting to change your mind. You are embarking on change. Be sure that you will like it.

An important part of the whole process of achieving mental toughness and the way to do so means that you will reach a half way point. You will have started to change and you will have some mental toughness but you will not feel you have changed much. Don´t worry about that. It will be an uncomfortable sensation overall because you will feel a lot of effort has been invested in changing and the results are not very great.

This is the make or break point. Here you will feel frustration and a little anger, but that is positive even if you don´t think so because it means you care about what is happening. Take stock of your new situation and look at the positives: You no longer want to smoke urgently, you have lost some weight, you can do a complete circuit at the gym, you can get up early without much effort. These are the signals that you are doing better. Learn to equate physical signs with mental results.

Now is the time to get your notebook out again and check the "before and after" list. Be honest with yourself and not overly critical. In your charts of getting up early, for example, you will now barely check because a new habit has become engrained: You now normally get up at 6 a.m. which you never did before. You have changed.

There will be other changes, perhaps you have decided you are going to be politer to strangers in a queue at the supermarket. You now automatically let other people come before you in the queue or you let others have your seat in the subway. These new things you do need to be repeated. This is a conscious effort that perseverance will make unconscious by dint of repetition.

Check your list of achievements and see which ones are now automatic. Is mindfulness becoming easier? Can you realistically visualize yourself as a success? Can you live with your success? This last is important. Most people who want to change the way they are, are not satisfied with themselves so they embark on change. But what happens when they actually change? Lots of them can´t live with their new selves.

They revert to type in the end because that is what they know best. This is a sad thing and you don´t want it to happen. Always bear in mind that you have consciously willed yourself to change and until it becomes second nature, you always run the risk of falling back to the way you used to be.

Keep your trusty notebook with your list of achievements and goals and read it daily, turn it into a mantra and repeat over and over again, analyze it, break it down into portions, digest it, consider the alternatives and make it part of you. By doing this, by becoming familiar with all the different aspects of yourself you will know yourself and your limitations so that willpower can be best used in the various aspects that need it.

Use affirmations. Make a list of the positives and repeat it to yourself. Focus on it. Make it part of your day to day living. Tell yourself you can do it. When you manage small goals on your way, stop and celebrate the milestones. Cheer yourself on and don´t berate yourself too much. Remember, you live with yourself all the time. You need to feel good about what is happening. So use your self-knowledge to cheer yourself on and remember that going backwards, giving up is not an option.

By using perseverance to whittle away the negative aspects of change, the reasons we procrastinate, give up, feel laziness and all the other somewhat tempting reasons to quit our quest for mental toughness, we get where we want to be. Others will eventually notice and this is like dieting, it takes a month for you to notice the change in your body, two months for your best friends to notice and three months for the rest of the world.

Another very important ally for perseverance is patience. Give yourself time. Don´t expect results to happen quickly. They will happen spottily, here a little success at getting up early, there a little loss of weight, a little further on easier cigarette resisting...

Meditate with your notebook and consider what you have achieved and the new you that is beginning to appear that says, "I don´t expect this to happen overnight", this realization which you didn´t really consider at the beginning, is proof of the new you. A patient you that realizes the amplitude of the undertaking.

This whole project is not about getting up early. It is about having a mind with a will, a disciplined mind that gets what it wants. It has taken a lot of preparation to get there and others will now consider you as one of those people that get what they want.

You have started to change. Don´t be afraid of change, of letting go that old you that procrastinated all the time, wasted time, didn´t focus on the job at hand, was a spendthrift, smoked, was overweight, out of shape, not particularly polite... All those things are part of the past. Keep them there just above the surface but stride on past them. They are not part of you now, or at least not so much because your new tools of perseverance and action with a little patience, have enabled you to move on.

Repeat over and over again your reasons for changing, the ultimate goal of why you want mental toughness. Understand what is going on and carry on with your focusing, visualizing. Use affirmative statements to help yourself. Affirmation is a sort of cover of your book of intents. Positive affirmation makes the whole process more real.

When you slip, when something doesn't work, use your new self to forgive and pick yourself up to carry on. Use your understanding to analyze why you failed this time and check that it is not a pattern you are creating like what happened in your old self. You don´t want to bring over bad habits in your new thinking processes.

Keep the good habits and eschew the bad ones. This involves realistic thinking and repetition of the good habits. Understanding the reasons for the bad ones and letting go of those reasons in favor of new ones will help you with the foundations of your pattern of thinking that will enable mental toughness.

A good mantra is "I don´t give up". Just like that, simple and short. Incorporate it into your daily living.

CHAPTER 4

MEDITATION, VISUALIZATION AND AFFIRMATION

Other ways of visualizing our future mental strength: Meditation, visualization and affirmation. When one puts together the Spartan approach to mental toughness from the Greco-Roman times along with millennial Eastern thinking as in meditation, one obtains a powerful combination that is bound to change anyone for the better. Indeed, using rote for memorizing mantras and thinking to foster mental toughness and inner strength in combination with meditation is a good thing. Use the best tools you can get from whatever the sources as long as they are ethical.

So, what is visualization? This is a sort of guided meditation in which you take stock of your assets and liabilities in your mind and visualize yourself as succeeding in any venture or solving any situation or problem. For example, you are a tennis player and you are learning how to serve with top spin. The teacher has explained and shown you how to do it and the class was earlier today and now it is bedtime. This is an ideal situation in which you lie down and carefully visualize in your mind all the elements of how to hit that top spin serve, you go through the motions in your mind in slow motion, feeling as precisely as possible how you did the stroke.

You then repeat it and try to be in your teacher's shoes while you observe yourself, you bring the racquet up, you toss the ball exactly the right height and you bring the racquet over your head until it hits the ball and you finish the stroke bringing the racquet up to your hip and move your foot forward with the impetus. This is visualization.

Another example: You lie in bed and try to find something you lost in the den. You carefully go over exactly what you were doing when you lost your fountain pen. You remember when you used it last. You retrace all the steps since you last saw it and there it is: it is in the breast pocket of your blazer which is on the back of the chair. You then sigh with relief. It was an expensive gold fountain pen your father gave you when you graduated.

Meditation with visualization can be a very powerful way to achieve things. If you meditate and make your mind go blank you can then visualize whatever situation or thing you need to solve. This is part of mental toughness. It is kind of fun to visualize in meditation. For example, you can do this fun thing: Think of someone you want to give a gift to who you love dearly. Meditate on this person. Get inside his or her mind and see things he or she cares about and then visualize yourself giving this person a special gift and visualize his or her reaction when presented with whatever you are giving.

Visualizing and meditation applied to strengthening mental toughness is not very hard once you have gotten into the habit of imposing discipline on yourself in other areas.

Affirmations

What are affirmations? These are those phrases people send you on your cell phone telling you things that are universal truths that get you smiling and feeling good. However, you don't have to import affirmations from famous people or friends of yours. You can create your own affirmations and these will be more powerful yet. An affirmation is a phrase that you repeat to yourself. You must use positive affirmations because if repeated enough, they tend to be true. For example, you can say "I am a hardworking person" and if you repeat it enough, you will start becoming a hardworking person.

The opposite is also true: "I am a lazy son of a gun". With enough repetition, this becomes true also, so you want to stay away from negative affirmations and stand by the positive ones. In a way, affirmations are really only just the appearance of mental toughness. The way it "looks". Once you are on your way to achieving the mental toughness basics that we started with, you embark on change and it will be natural to think "I am a hardworking person" why? Because mental toughness has made you a hardworking person so it is almost irrelevant to call yourself one. However, watch out because in the beginning, it is important to give yourself doses of "I am a genius" or "I am better today than I was yesterday".

Because with the other tools you have in your box of mental toughness elements, affirmations are the doses of positive thinking you need to get the machine working, the machine, by the way, is your mind.

Visualizing the person you will be in the future is a great way to set the master plan for your unique approach to self-improvement and affirmations that you can believe in will eventually be true and second nature to you. See? You are already changing! Change is like when it is dawn. Very little by little things in the dark start having shapes and colors, and before you know it, they are standing out there in the broad daylight of your conscious awareness. This is heady stuff but it is going to happen to you very gradually and like most things that happen gradually, they will stick for good.

Affirmations like "I can do whatever I set my mind to" will serve you in the long-term task of mental toughness.

Take out your notebook and sit down and write ten affirmation phrases that apply to you personally. These are going to be your mantras and take them one at a time and visualize what they mean to you. For example, problem solving. Let's say your affirmation is "I can do whatever I set my mind to", visualize yourself in a difficult situation saying this and see what happens. You will see yourself calm in the middle of chaos, focusing on the task at hand and succeeding. This is what you need to do with affirmations. Keep them around, think about them, make a list of them and read it often. In fact, you should keep a diary of all the things to do with your search for mental toughness and go over it. See how you have changed in some ways and use that to map out the future of your change process. Mental toughness is not a rigid thing, it is flexible and it grows as your inner self grows and be proud to see how far you have come since you started once you have mastered some of the things mentioned in this book.

Make yourself a wish list of mental toughness elements and use visualization to visualize yourself fulfilling the wish. It is not wishful thinking it is making wishes come true and you can do this with visualization and affirmation.

Affirmations are things we tell ourselves or that others have told us that we believe in. For example, your parents. Most people have parents that are kind of judgmental. They will say: "Billy is pigheaded", "Sally is thoughtful and is generous to a fault". Billy and Sally grew up with parents saying things like this all the time and they became that way.

This is not to say that it is bad for parents to say things about their children but it will make the children be what the parent says and this can have tragic results, think of people that you may know that grew up with parents or teachers saying things like "he will never be good at anything, bone lazy". Whoever got labeled that, has a heavy load to bear. But whatever you may have been called or branded as, with affirmations you can change all of that by choosing to say something different about yourself, for example: "rather lazy but extremely creative". This will counterbalance anything said in the past about you.

Choose affirmations that will help you in your search for mental toughness. "Prettiest girl in the family" is not a very useful affirmation but "I am intelligent and will be a success at whatever I choose to do" is more in line with developing mental toughness to become mentally strong.

You can even say "I am mentally strong and have lots of mental toughness". If you do, it will be easier for you to become mentally strong with willpower and this new mantra in your life. Write it down several times in your notebook. It will be something you can look back on later on when you have a weak point and have slipped a little.

You want to watch out for failure, this is when you give in to old mindsets and habits. This will happen because changing is not like wearing a different set of clothes. It is more like when a pet sheds its fur and new fur grows. When this happens, you can´t really tell where the old fur is and where the new fur has grown, the pet, a cat, for example, sheds its old fur in the summer and at the same time new fur grows so the cat is never totally without fur or totally with new fur, likewise, you won´t become totally different and full of mental toughness and strength from one day to the next, this isn´t even desirable. You will change gradually and one day you will look back and read your notebook and say, "wait a moment... this was when... it was two years ago!" and then you will see how much you have changed.

The secret is not to expect any change to happen quickly, sure there will be moments of self-realization, of Zen like insight of the future you but like all of the most solid things on Earth, change is best when it is gradual, anchored in you, a solid belief that is unshakeable because it has been acquired with time and effort.

Visualize yourself in the future

You don´t have to be harsh on yourself. Give yourself rewards, not excessive ones but a prize now and then to make the hard parts more palatable and easier to get through.

If part of your quest for mental toughness has to do with dieting, then reward yourself with something every time you manage to keep five lbs. off every month, for example, something to wear that enhances your thinner figure.

If what you are after is to quit smoking for good, every month that you did not smoke, give yourself a gift worth five packs of cigarettes. This reward is part of your self-discipline. You need to help yourself along on the path to mental strength. Just sit back and say to yourself "one day I won´t need to do all of this because I will have changed the way I want to change". This is true and seeing the broader picture at the end of the journey helps with the indecision, the procrastination, the laziness, the disappointment when slipping. If you know that "this too will one day pass", then you are set for success.

So, in sum, meditating on affirmative statements can be a great way to start the day when you get up early just because you are becoming more disciplined.
Turn yourself into your greatest asset because in the end, all you have is you, so be sure to make you be on your side!
Self-discipline means renouncement, it means giving up, what? Giving up all those deadweight ideas that were immobilizing you and keeping you from reaching the goals you wanted to reach.

Visualizing yourself in the process of attaining your goals helps reach them. Use your imagination to be who you really want to be, but make sure that the person you want to be is really you and not the expectation of others.

Write down the affirmations that you want, not some list that others tell you. You decide what you want in life. And you are totally responsible for that so make sure you want something that is worth it.

CHAPTER 5

MENTAL TOUGHNESS TECHNIQUES

In chapter 1 we mentioned the source of mental toughness; it came from pedagogues of the Greco-Roman era and these teachers had the idea of making their pupils stronger and more ethical people by means of academic discipline in areas such as rhetoric, mathematics, astronomy, music, geometry, grammar and logic.

Later on, we mentioned mindfulness which is being in the here and now. Most of the time, we occupy our minds with other things and just put in the motions when doing what we are doing now. With mindfulness, you are disciplining your mind to be consciously aware of what is happening right now. There is an explanation for why mindfulness is kind of hard and this is that the brain once it has learned something, does that thing automatically as much as possible. This is the reason you cannot remember every single instant of what you did yesterday, if you could, you would never get anything done or do anything because you would be flooded by mental images of all the things you have done all these days and years of your existence so the brain obviates most of the things which you do automatically. This is the scientific explanation but this does not mean that mindfulness is not a good thing. It is a very valuable tool in mental toughness so use it.

We also mentioned willpower, this is crucial and it is necessary to develop your willpower if you want to get anywhere at all in having mental toughness. Willpower is the number one tool in getting you started and on the right track. Willpower is what you need for all the aspects of the job of mentally disciplining yourself into success. You will need it to do almost anything you want to learn. You must force yourself into making new mental routes in your brain by repetition and this will gall you and you will find yourself being extremely unwilling to even start and willpower, the wish to succeed, the ardent desire to learn and get out of your comfort zone and enter the area of what you do not know or that grey area where you suffer because of whatever you are trying to achieve, think of sweating in the gym while your body groans and wants to go to the shower, think of getting up early in winter when it is still dark and what you crave is another hour in your bed, think of having to resist one more cigarette right after you resisted one, your mind will be telling you that what you want is to just go and have that smoke, but you won´t.

Meditation is another thing we went over. The calm way of contemplating what is going on inside you and staying focused on one thought while you calm your mind and get it where you want it to be. Meditation is necessary for mental toughness if only because once you master meditation, you will be on the way to mastering a mental toughness. Think of meditation as a tool that measures your progress with mental toughness as the final result.

When you start meditating correctly, you will notice it, it will be easy to slip into that special groove that has you in a trance like a state while you think of Vacuity or whatever it is that you think about while meditating. Once the meditation starts working, all the other aspects will have started changing too.

Self-discipline, this is knowing how far you can bend in one way or another and still stay on track. Self-discipline will be your guideline in not cheating and abiding by the master plan which is to achieve mental toughness. You have to have a certain degree of motivation and discipline to start with. A good way to know if you do is to be sure that what you really want is mental toughness. One thing is for sure, mental toughness is not easy to come by. Just reading this book will not be enough, you will need to actually get out there with your notebook, make your lists, get up early, have cold showers, refrain from smoking, keep from raiding the fridge in search of comfort foods at night. Only by having a little self-discipline you will be able to embark on the rest of the things. You must have a certain degree of self-knowledge, know your weak spots and your strong ones and use that knowledge to mature in a certain way, don´t be hedonistic and do be disciplined.

Self-discipline is a cousin of Attitude: The right attitude will get you farther ahead than you might believe. You have to have the right attitude or else nothing in this book will serve you and you might as well give up and go back to bed because if your attitude is not right, then nothing and nobody will serve you.

Change: In chapter 1 we talked about change. Change is the mysterious result in the end, what happens when we change? We no longer are the same as we used to be and people who have used mental toughness become different, they become their own creators. They do not depend on others and they are not afraid of change because that is what this is all about in the end, ultimately, you in your quest for self-discipline will have changed. It is important to shed your old self gradually as you incorporate things of your new self.

One important element in change is a failure: We mention it here because failure is going back to the way you used to be, the way that got you where you were before you decided to read this book and change. Failure is horrible but it is doable, you can get over it and progress. Knowing it is out there ready to undermine all your achievements is a good thing because that way you can avoid it and when you can´t, you can overcome it, you can get up again and carry on, tears and bruises included. Failure is logical because you are only human and this isn´t about being super human. That is one of the reasons why you need to include discomfort and pain in the parcel. If you are afraid of discomfort you will never be able to recover from failure because you will give in at the very first sign of discomfort. So, add failure to your set of tools if only to be aware of it.

Experience: This one is similar to attitude and self-discipline, you need to gain experience and etch new things in your brain, you must mature, grow and experience new things that you incorporate into your mind.

Rote learning: This one is very rudimentary. By dint of repetition you have learned many things in life, most things are learned by repetition particularly in sports and less so in things like art or music which are more intuitive but repetition is necessary to learn anything and the greatest musicians or singers or painters had to learn and repeat over and over again the basics of their art until they mastered it completely and could branch out into other areas of their art that no longer require repetition. In chapter 1 we talked about rote learning, the humble tool of over and over again things. Don´t discard it ever. It will serve you in any future moment when faced with something new, you will master whatever new thing comes along by repetition.

In chapter 2 we considered exercise, this is the material way in which repetition is done. We repeat things over and over again to exercise the mind. Exercise can be made easier with mindfulness. Remember, in your quest for a more disciplined mind, you do not have to do everything with grim determination, give yourself a break and use your imagination to do all the things you need to do to achieve your goal. Smile. You can do it.

Focus was another thing. Focus is light weight mindfulness, it is a long-term kind of mindfulness in which you stay in the right direction on your journey towards perfection in this project of mental toughness. Staying focused is staying concentrated. You can´t do it all the time but focusing is easier than mindfulness or meditation, use your concentration to focus and at the same time use focusing to stay on track while meditating or using mindfulness to exercise your mind.

Visualization was another thing we considered in chapter 2. Visualization is how you are going to use your meditation and mindfulness to get mental toughness in a visual way. With visualization, you imagine and view in your mind exactly what is going to happen to you as you practice your meditation and mindfulness.

In chapter 2 we considered emotions. These are part of the mind. You are a human being with a soul and you feel things. This is natural and you should not be afraid of feelings. Mental toughness comes with compassion, love, honesty, charity and all the other emotions that make up a human being.

In chapter 3 we considered perseverance and action. Stick with it and watch things start to happen! Perseverance is willpower in action, your mind making the right moves and you do the things you need to do to get where you want to go.

We also talked about affirmations. These are your personal phrases and mantras that put into a phrase the whole philosophy of what you want to do with your mind.

When I had cancer, my sister gave me a thing called an "affirmation ball". This was a joke item with a window and in it phrases appeared like "You will succeed", "You are the best", etc. It was a laugh but those phrases helped me get over a very scary situation. I still have my affirmation ball somewhere but I developed my own personal affirmations and these help me today. Affirmations can be vague and general or specific and concrete. I like to make my own ones because they portray me as a person in my own special way and you can find your own phrases and repeat them. Just like people say "Oh, I´m too stupid to learn a language" and they never do, you can say "I will succeed in my quest for inner knowledge" or "I can beat the habit" or "practice makes perfect". Go to your notebook and consider the ten affirmations you wrote down and see if any have changed and write new ones to suit your new self.

In chapter 4 we considered changing as an ongoing process that never ends and we had an example of a cat or dog that sheds hair but is never completely fur-less, as old hairs are shed, new ones replace them so the pet is never the same, it is constantly changing but you can´t tell really when it is finished molting. You will "molt" too. If you keep your notebook, at the end of a year since you started, you can go back and see which of the things about you and your quest for mental toughness have changed. People never really change, they "morph" and become different very gradually, mostly it is time that effects the change but some people can change with the aid of their mind, their willpower and their mental toughness. Finally, the last consideration, "know yourself" this was an affirmation of the Greeks. By knowing yourself, you can know how reliable you will be in a difficult moment. Mental toughness requires hard work and knowing your strengths and failings is crucial for mapping out your plan for achieving the final results.

Reward yourself when reaching goals and milestones. Remember to be your own best friend because if you do not believe in yourself, who is going to believe in you? Will you be able to believe that other person? Mental toughness is a plan in action, not a final result.

CHAPTER 6

FLEXING THE MIND

Firstly, congratulations for having got this far. What comes next is for people who have done the exercises and suggestions in the previous chapters and who have dedicated thought and time to the concepts discussed. People who have made lists and filled out grids in their quest for mental toughness will now be ready for whatever life puts in their path as an obstacle, a concept, a new element or simply something unknown to them heretofore. You will now have all the elements you need in order to succeed.

However, it is necessary to utilize your hard-earned knowledge about yourself and your mind and practice.
Remember your old trusty notebook? Now is the time to go back and review those first entries you made in it. Use your visualization skills to remember and put yourself for a moment where you were that very first day

you decided to get up at 6 a.m. in an effort to start being more disciplined. Now that time has gone by and it is almost second nature to you to get up at that time, you may smile reflectively when considering your old self and comparing it to the new one.

This chapter is about doing that, comparing the old with the new. Go ahead, check out your old self and your new one. If you were dieting and fasting and having a hard time getting through the day without longing after a donut or some peanuts or a slice of pizza, now that you no longer have those cravings and have lost the weight you wanted, read about what it was like when this was a crucial issue in your life and you were miserable because you were slipping and sliding all over the place, but no, you carried on, you persevered and today you have a trimmer figure and most of all, you don´t have those awful cravings. You have achieved a major milestone in your plan for mental toughness and curiously, those things that you thought were hard and tough mental goals are almost easy today.

Check out the grids you did when doing mindfulness and jerking your mind back to the task over and over again, now you can put yourself to sleep by visualizing each muscle in your body and it takes you thirty minutes.

Procrastination is a word that does not exist in your vocabulary today, but, check that notebook to see what the baby steps were like when you used all your willpower to get your shoes on to walk the dog on those wintery nights back from work.

You can visualize any scenario nowadays because of all the practice you put in visualizing when you started your search for mental toughness. You listen to music in a different way, logical thinking is not a mystery to you.

You have changed and now you want to stay this new way, rather, you want to continue changing but in your own personal direction. You have mastered the art of patience and change. A few people out there that you know come to you for advice. They take what you have to say into consideration. You are a respected person in your circle and in your neighborhood, people consider you to be polite, kind, compassionate and loving.

Now is the time to move the whole thing up a level. Meditate with more concentration, visualize things in your life in greater detail.

Take another notebook and write down all your achievements ever since the last entry in your old notebook. Put the old one away and forget about it for a little while as you start the new one. This new notebook is your new you. The you that has mental toughness. The you that can effectively meditate and visualize. The you that has seemingly endless willpower and the you that no longer need to use that willpower for simple things like getting out of bed in the mornings.

Practice all the things in this book and repeat them. Now you have enough self-knowledge to be able to do all the exercises without faltering.

Do you now do your mindfulness for an hour every morning first thing in the morning? Now you get up early and incorporate this hour of being with yourself as an automatic thing that is part of you. Your family may or may not know that you do this but for you, it is second nature. You enter a "Zen" like state when meditating and you are conscious of every muscle and bone in your body as you go to bed and relax the muscles in your body to achieve rest.

You are like a body builder, you have intimate knowledge of your mind and how it works. You are a specialist in your mind and finally, yes, you have mental toughness.

But you need to perfect it. Use it or lose it and you aren´t a quitter or a waster.

Now what you can do is move on and practice all the things you have learned in this book in order to make sure that you don´t forget them.

If you were a dieter and now you have shed those extra pounds, you now know what to do and what not do in terms of dieting and in your cupboard, there are no snacks, your refrigerator does not hide bottles and cans of soft drinks. You are past that. Stay that way or better yet, make your body even better by going to a gym if you haven´t already added that to your set of tools.

If you were a smoker, revel now in the wonderful sensation of no cigarette smoke and smells in your home or your clothes. You no longer have to buy yourself presents every month because you are rewarding yourself for not smoking. But remember, as an ex-smoker you can have a relapse, but your mindfulness and your mental toughness will ensure that you will not have a relapse.

Remember failure lurking around at every bend in the road? Well, it is still there but by now you have enough tools to be able to avert it. You will know how to react to failure, you basically do as you have always done, get up, brush yourself off and get back into the field and carry on.

Funnily enough, a curious thing happens, you now do not need so much willpower to achieve things, you don´t need to use affirmative statements so much, these things are now second nature to you. Mental toughness? This is an integral part of who you are!

It wasn´t easy to get here but you have arrived, in a way, you have always been here... Remember the pet shedding hairs? You have shed hairs and grown a new pelt of wisdom that you were not aware of.

Go back and get your old notebook. Read it and check out the old you and the new you. Find the exercises that were hardest for you, the failings that aggravated you the most and read them, use your mindfulness and your visualization abilities to go back to those gray days in which you thought you would never make it and see what you did right.

Use that old element, patience, to proceed into the future.

Bodybuilders perfect their sculpted figures with time and effort. They are a shining example of what the human mind can do to achieve perfection but people searching for mental toughness are in a totally different league, they are the bodybuilders of the mind.

Make sure that you continue flexing your mind with all the encounters life puts in your path and remember to pat yourself on the back every now and then because you are still you and you need rewards. You have changed but the change has been gradual and a certain amount of time has gone by. People like your parents will say "he or she has matured", that is their way of noticing how you have changed, smile and let them think it is that, you know that it is partially true. You are your own self-made person.

A new undertaking could be considering others, reaching out to others to help them, remember, emotions are out there too, compassion is one of them and people who have self-discipline have uncluttered their minds and done away with a lot of trivia and rubbish in order to make room for things that really count like love and compassion. Exert those, use your mental toughness to help others. That is what love is about.

See? You started by wanting to be a super human person immured to common failings and what have you become? You are a superior being in comparison to your old self, you are no longer afraid of suffering, of losing, of failing, your brain has calluses because of all the times you failed and got right back up again.

One thing you don´t notice too much is people who admire you because you consistently eat salads instead of pizza portions and fried chicken at lunch because you want to stay fit and trim. People say you have a will of iron...

Your new mind is shining through the layer of oldness. You now are able to do things that back then before you embarked on mental toughness, you thought was not feasible. You really don´t need any reminders to do anything more so find something new to do and incorporate all the techniques and concepts discussed in this book to your new life and carry on. You have succeeded and now you want to stay that way and it is not necessary to suffer and use the herculean strength of willpower to stay where you are. It is a strange thing but all those people out there using mental toughness need it less and less as they progress because the mind has carved out new habits in the brain and these new habits have finally replaced the old habits that were so hard to change at the very beginning. This is the secret. You have finally created a new you that does not need a lot of effort to maintain. Stay that way. Now you can reach out to others and help them achieve their goals. You can be a mentor to a few people in your personal circle or at work or in college or wherever you may be.

Consider yourself to be a success but we know that you never really considered this part of the quest as a goal, it isn´t it is simply a sweet place to be that you have earned for yourself and since you have learned to be your own best friend, congratulate yourself and go out there and have yourself a treat.

About those notebooks. Keep them. People who succeed in life never forget where they came from and where they are heading for. Follow your own counsel and don´t forget to meditate, visualize, affirm and use your willpower to stay where you are as you set out for the next quest in your life.

You are now a person with true mental toughness and it isn´t a titanic task. You can visualize yourself in any situation and know what you need to do because you know yourself truly. Keep the old parts of you that got you where you are, those basic things that you already had when you started, they are your past and they must help you enter your future.

Enjoy the perks of not being a mental weakling but help others that are not as fortunate as you are because someone helped you become who you are now. That, someone, was you. The you that you are now is someone that has been at your side inside your mind from the very beginning.

Use your mental toughness to explore more regions of your mind, use mindfulness, visualizations, affirmations, willpower, repetition and meditation to guide you wherever you go next.

BONUS CHAPTERS FROM MY BOOKS

EMPATH

CHAPTER 2

The Fundamentals of Emotions: How they affect us in our everyday lives, what to do about them, and why it matters

Understanding the empathic power is like understanding a machine. You have to understand its parts. You may be able to drive a car, but unless you understand how the gas pump, pistons, axels, or battery work together to make the car go vroom, you're no mechanic. The best mechanic knows every single part of a car and how it fits together in order to make the car perform. The same goes for skills. Practitioners of martial arts don't start learning flying spin kicks right off the bat. They first learn basics. These can be as simple as proper stance, to doing push-ups. Until you learn all the parts of the specific discipline you cannot possible master it. The same goes for the Empath. One must learn all the parts of being an empath before they can master it to its true potential.

"I know what emotions are" I hear you snicker in the back of your mind. And I can't disagree with you. We are taught about emotions from an early age. How to recognize them, replicate them, and which ones are appropriate for which situations. Emotions are behind most of our decisions, and ideologies. They act as a driving force for our will and serve as a connection to the things we like and the people we love. But de we really understand emotion? Do we ever consider where it comes from, or why emotions exist? Do we ever ask why some people feel certain emotions in a situation while others feel differently? Do we ever consider feelings to an extreme that we have never felt before? Is the spectrum of feelings as finite as we are taught as children? Cataloging and experiencing emotions and feelings is something most humans are capable of and is no small feat in and of itself. The consideration of them as power and the effect emotions have on us as a species and acting to harness that power for the greater good is what leads to understanding the powers of the Empath. So, let's begin considering.

The most obvious observation one can make is that emotions effect people every day. They can cause an angry person to assault someone or a happy person to buy alcohol for an entire bar. Emotions seem to be a driving force for many human behaviors. Yet when someone acts hyper emotionally, such as crying or screaming, we chide them for being irrational. From this we get the main effect of emotions on humans, emotions cause humans to think irrationally. This is perceived as a negative today. Someone in an intense emotional state might be too scared to run for their life, or too sad to help someone. As a result, we are taught (and teach our children) to ignore emotions and think rationally. However, this assumption is false. Though some people act irrationally out of emotions, others use their emotions to heighten their perceptions or performances. Many athletes state that they "hate" their opponents during a match or game, only to be courteous and sportsmanlike. The point I want to make is this; Though emotions do have the potential to sway our rational thoughts, humans need emotions to connect with others in a meaningful way, which is essential to being human. Instead of trying to subdue our emotions we need to learn how to integrate our emotions into our rational thoughts. To be an Empath means to have full access to your emotions as well as the emotions of others without the loss of common sense. But when one is taught by an early age to think critically without emotion, how can one learn to experience rational emotion? Fear not, there are ways to reteach your brain to think in an emotionally enlightened way. It starts with something known as emotional intelligence.

According to Wikipedia (which gives the best definition) someone with a high emotional intelligence can ".... adequately recognize their own emotions and those of others, discern between different feelings and label them appropriately, use emotional information to guide thinking and behavior, and manage and/or adjust emotions to adapt to environments or achieve one's goal(s)". As we discussed, many people are taught how to discern and label emotions. What we are interested in especially as Empaths, is using emotions to guide thinking and behavior. Again, there will be a split between the people who have already untapped their empathic ability and those who have not. For those of you who have taken the time to master your emotional intelligence, congratulations. You can skim through the rest of this chapter and see if there is anything of interest. For those of you who haven't, I have good news for you. I'll give you a simple checklist of three exercises that can be used to raise your emotional intelligence starting today.

The Emotional Intelligence Training Check List. Do These Every Day!

1.	Self Reflection: Take some time at the end of your day and think about the events. Write them out if it helps you remember anything. Consider all the emotions you felt. Did you get angry? Sad? Was there something that overjoyed you? Remember these events and reflect on the why. Why did said event make you mad, or happy? What would have made the situation different? How could you have made the situation different? Could you have made a bad situation good just by putting on a smile? Did you really have to argue with the guy about the parking spot, could you have controlled your anger in hopes that he would control his? As odd as it sounds you can even ask a friend, or significant other to help with your reflections. Sometimes asking others for their perspective on certain situations is the best way to get an accurate reflection of how you express your emotions, as well as give you a perspective into other's emotions. This is the most important one, it is also the hardest, but keeping it up is the quickest way to boost your emotional intelligence.

2. Always consider others' perspectives: This one is more of a mindset than an exercise, but it is important in Emotional Intelligence and Empathy just the same. When ever you interact with someone, try to look at things from their point of view. I know this one is taught a lot, but I'm dreadfully surprised at all the people I know and meet who fail at this, so I'll say it here. Sometimes its easy to see something from someone else's point of view but other times it is hard, especially if you have just had a confrontation with the person. Whatever the situation, do your best to take a deep breath,

count to ten, and consider the situation from the viewpoint of the other parties involved. After a while it will become second nature.

3. Talk to people. This one seems a little silly. We talk to people every day, and yet we don't all become emotional experts. But that's only because we aren't talking the right way, or in a way that stimulates our emotional intelligence. The only way to grow emotionally through talking to humans is by talking about emotions. Do you have unresolved feelings for someone? A crush or maybe someone offended you? Tell them. Hopefully you and the other person can have a discussion and resolve your feelings. Don't understand why someone is upset with you? Ask them about it. Whether you end up seeing eye to eye or not (while sad) may be irrelevant depending on the circumstance. What is important is taking a step to

understanding the emotions of others in the context of yourself and the world.

So now you know the effect of emotions, and what to do to integrate them into your rational mind, which is important to grow your Empathic abilities.
As we discovered in chapter 1, an empath is someone who can comprehend and feel the emotions of others. Cultivating strong emotional intelligence is an important key in this regard. Once you have gained enough experience with your rational emotions, you will be able to consider peoples' point of views effortlessly. The perception of other peoples' viewpoints, how an empath can "see from all sides" and know what people are feeling, and if you can extend that feeling rationally then getting a glimpse into the thoughts of an individual becomes a much easier feat. When you have really mastered

this aspect of Empathy, you will start to feel peoples' emotions as if you were experiencing the sensations yourself.

Many years ago, when I was still in college, I lived in a boarding house with 5 roommates. By now I had realized that I was more emotionally perceptive than others and started researching Empaths. One of my roommates came home, we'll call him Mate. He rushed up to his room, which was a little past mine. He waved at me and entered. Me, being bored, went to go see what he was up to. Per form, Mate was playing Grand Theft Auto on his PlayStation 3, but he didn't appear to be having a blast like he always does. There was some sort of darkness around him. "What's wrong?" I asked him. He looked at me with some surprise. "Nothing is wrong, I'm just playing video games" He kept playing. For some reason I could tell he was lying, he just didn't seem right. I could feel his despair. "Mate, you can tell me, I won't judge you" I sat next to him and looked at him. After a minute Mate put the controller down and looked at me. "I've been doing heroin, I think my mom knows and my sister said I can't see my nephew if I don't get clean!" He started crying. I had no idea that this was the bomb that Mate was gonna drop on me. I thought to myself "Well duh, just get clean," but as he sat there silently sobbing my heart softened a bit and I had a different thought. "Why is it he started it in the first place?" I knew Mate's upbringing, we grew up about 30 miles apart, me in a small town, him from a small city, a small city that had a terrible reputation. The crime rate in that city is the highest in the state. The poverty rate is high as well, and as you can probably guess the school was terrible. High school is were Mate first tried pills such as oxytocin, which would eventually lead to his heroin addiction. Even when he moved out he would always be around these people. They were all he knew. I felt for him, but even though I felt for him I knew there was only one rational solution. "Man, I know this sucks, but you have to go to rehab." The next week Mate was booked in a 6-month rehab. I dropped him off. Once he completed it he joined the army. I haven't talked to him since, but I message him on Facebook now and then and try to like the photos he takes with his nephew.

Made in the USA
San Bernardino, CA
21 January 2019